THE MYTH BUSTER SERIES #1

Conflict Is Bad and Should Be Avoided!

How to Treasure Difficult Conversations

Carol Diane

Copyright © 2025 by Carol Diane

ISBN 978-1-943627-09-7

All rights reserved. No part of this publication may be reproduced, distributed, or transmitted in any form or by any means, including photocopying, recording, or other electronic or mechanical methods, without the prior written permission of the author, except in the case of brief quotations embodied in reviews and other noncommercial uses permitted by copyright law.

The Myth Buster Series belongs to the nonfiction self-help genre, but in the case studies, all names and identifying personal characteristics have been changed to disguise identities. Consequently, any resemblance to persons living or dead is entirely coincidental and unintentional. The information provided in this series is for educational purposes only, and is never intended to tell anyone what to do in a specific situation. The author makes no warranties or representations, express or implied, about the suitability or reliability of the information for any purpose, and disclaims all liability for errors or omissions and for any consequence arising from the use of the information herein.

Scripture quotations are taken from *The NIV Study Bible*, The Zondervan Corporation, 1995, Grand Rapids, Michigan.

THE MYTH BUSTER SERIES
Introduction

If we're not careful, we can pick up some harmful ideas in our society, and we can get hurt as a result. Maybe we don't yet think of ourselves as "hurt." Maybe we'd just say "frustrated." Or maybe we'd say we feel "trapped." Or maybe we'd just say we're not finding enough satisfaction in life.

Often, a wrong idea infiltrates our society after originating in the painful childhoods of many people. These children develop their philosophies in reaction to the dysfunction at home, and then they spread their maladaptive philosophy to others. These ideas can spread throughout the culture and can be handed down from generation to generation.

I call these wrong ideas "myths." That word seems appropriate because of the two definitions of the word "myth":

1. a story handed down
2. a widely held but false idea.

With these two definitions in mind, we need to realize that the myths in this series are hazardous to your health and happiness. They can lead to tremendous emotional pain. Many people cling to these beliefs and preach them to others, perhaps even demand that others adhere to these beliefs and act accordingly. But these ideas are all harmful over-generalizations. The destruction they cause in families and other groups can be severe and widespread, and still, some people would rather see their lives destroyed than admit that their favorite myth is a lie or an over-simplification.

The ideas in this series come from several sources. One is my life experience and the lives of people I've known. I've seen the kind of destruction these myths can cause. I've experienced the damage myself, and so I've been emotionally involved. But I've also been an analytical observer from the outside.

A second important source is my master's training in counseling, especially the family systems training. Families and people in general show a variety of common patterns or traits. That makes sense because, after all, people are people! And we're not perfect—we have our flaws, right? But we can be a work-in-progress. And we can feel a great sense of relief and relaxation when we accept the fact that we are just a work-in-progress, and we truly understand:

- that's okay
- that's good enough
- that's all that's possible
- and we are lovable and loved even with our flaws.

A third source for me personally is a growing understanding of God and the universal principles at work in this world. I've learned the hard way to look for Wisdom and save myself from experiencing so much trouble in life.

All of the case studies in this series are true, but the names and other identifying details have been changed. Some case studies are used to show extreme examples—the places to which a myth can lead us if we've drifted way down the wrong path.

Each book in the series starts with an extreme case. Then you can ask yourself whether you or someone you know displays any of those tendencies, perhaps to a lesser degree. Because we're human, all of us can tend to respond at least a little bit like the individual in our extreme example.

All of the information presented here is meant to help you avoid the misery that so many others have experienced. Now, finally, you can free yourself and move forward to create your best life possible.

Ancient scripture offers this advice:

> Enter through the narrow gate. For wide is the gate and broad is the road that leads to destruction, and many enter through it. But small is the gate and narrow the road that leads to life, and only a few find it.

Many people approach life without thinking very deeply about it. They mindlessly repeat whatever they've been taught. They go through the motions. And then they lament the misery in which they find themselves. They've wandered with the crowds through the wide gate and down the broad road.

You can decide to be courageous enough to look with new eyes and find a better path. Here at Happiness Reclaimed, we prefer dealing with truth and finding real answers to life's challenges. Dealing with truth sometimes requires extra work up front, but the payoff for us is worth it.

So it's time to dispel a few myths. Let's head for the Narrow Gate.

Questions: Introduction

1. Prior to reading this book, had you thought of yourself as a work-in-progress? How do you feel about the idea of being a work-in-progress?

2. What are the alternatives to accepting yourself as a work-in-progress?

3. What specifically would you wish to see changed in your life?

4. If a miracle happened and those changes occurred instantly, how would you know? What would you observe as different? And how would you BE different?

5. Which parts of your answers to #3 and #4 are within your control?

The Path of Misery: Barry

Barry grew up in a tense environment. His parents would argue at home, and he also discovered that any attempt within the family to discuss feelings was met with criticism, blame, or some other negative reaction. He was also picked on and teased within the family. This sweet little boy with high intelligence and tender feelings was trapped in a world that constantly caused him anxiety and even fear. As you might have guessed, he learned conflict avoidance at an early age. He learned it so well that it was seared into his personality.

The most common result could be seen in this typical interaction decades later. One day, he felt heartbroken to learn that his parents had thrown away all the negatives for the family photos, and this was of course before the days of digital cameras and the technology commonly used to duplicate photos.

Looking at family pictures was one of the few ways Barry could connect emotionally to his family, and in those days, the negatives were the way for him to have copies of his own.

"You pitched them?" he wailed, unable to mask his feelings of hurt and disappointment.

"Well, you couldn't see what was on them anyway!" his mom snarled.

That was the end of that. His mom's implication that negatives had no value would stand. Her ignorance about them would go unchallenged. Barry's upset feelings would never be acknowledged. The significance he attached to photos would never be explained. His deepest feelings about his family would stay locked away forever.

Barry had indeed learned that conflict is to be avoided, even feared. Hurt feelings are best left unspoken. Disagreements are best stifled. Differing opinions are best hidden. Anything that could rock the boat should be stuffed deep, deep down where it can be forgotten—or so he hopes.

The philosophy that Barry formed as a child was a survival strategy and produced a kind of safety in his family of origin, but now it is destroying his life as an adult. His habit of conflict avoidance isolates him in a world in which honesty or emotional intimacy is impossible. And that's a lonely place to be.

When he has an opinion or a desire or a need, he usually doesn't feel safe to share it—not if there is any chance the other person will disagree or disapprove. He is therefore trapped and powerless, isolated and unknown, a victim of his own philosophy about how he should conduct himself.

But opinions and desires and needs have a way of persisting, and the pressure builds. So Barry decides to get what he wants behind the backs of others.

At work, he agrees to doing things a certain way. But his coworkers later discover he did it HIS way behind their back. He makes all kinds of promises to his wife, but breaks many of them for any number of reasons.

Barry will do anything to avoid the anxiety he feels when a potential conflict or difference of opinion appears. And yet, he is also determined to have things his way. So he misleads people, and what he wants is most often attained secretly, and at the expense of someone else. He has lost the ability to care about the rights of others.

He sees himself as only doing what's right and fair. He can't see, or chooses not to see, that he misleads others and then betrays their trust—and that's a horrible thing to do.

Instead of seeing how he mistreats others, he sees himself as the victim and sees others as all-powerful and controlling for daring to ask something of him. His resentment toward others builds. After all, they're the problem, right? They don't think as he thinks. They don't want what he wants. And they possess this mysterious power to control and intimidate—or so he thinks.

His anger grows on a foundation of long-repressed rage for his parents. But he can't express those feelings because, remember, he learned long ago that expressing feelings is too dangerous. So the anger goes underground and he turns to a subtle form of revenge called passive-aggressive behavior.

Barry finds subtle ways of hurting people, taking out his frustrations and anger on them. But again, he can never admit to anyone—maybe not even himself—what he's doing. So he pretends his bad behavior is accidental. His mantras become "I didn't know" and "I forgot."

"I didn't know that would cause you so much pain."

"I forgot you don't like that."

"I'm just clueless," he says.

That may or may not be true, depending upon how sick and unaware Barry is. Some people at least temporarily lack the ability to examine themselves and see what's happening inside their hearts and minds.

But Barry sometimes admits that his motivation for hurtful behavior is the resentment he feels. At those times, he is most definitely aware of his cruelty, and he believes in his heart that he's justified. His anger blinds him, just as anger can temporarily blind us all.

Of course, the greatest irony of Barry's story is that, by trying so hard to avoid conflict, Barry ends up creating way more conflict than ever! This is what myths are like. To put it bluntly, they lead to insanity. Wouldn't you agree? Isn't it insane to be so conflict-averse that you end up creating greater amounts of conflict?

That's what you need to understand about myths. They actually backfire. They actually are counterproductive. They actually take you farther away from what you really want. They lure you with an illusion of safety and relief, but they can lead ultimately to a hellish existence.

! ! ! ! ! *Passive aggression and cruelty*

Barry is just one example of how people can drift into passive aggression and other forms of hurtful behavior. His inability to face and heal from his own childhood pain created a blockage of the heart, not a physical blockage, but an inability to see and feel the pain of others—or even worse, a tendency to enjoy the pain of others. Counseling could help him become appropriately assertive or face conflict in a productive way—if only he could see he needed help.

Barry is an extreme case, but not as rare as some people might think. You may know someone a little like Barry. If you see just a bit of Barry in yourself, congratulations! It's an encouraging sign that you can see truth rather than cling to denial, because now you have a chance to pivot. I've known others who took a good look at themselves and then changed direction.

!!!! A habit of lying

Some conflict avoiders may not be cruel or passive-aggressive, but they might just develop a lying habit in order to avoid the displeasure of others.

!!! Depression

An even larger number of people do none of these things, but are simply trapped in the habit of being passive and withholding their true thoughts and feelings. They freely admit they fear conflict and say nothing when a sticky situation arises. For some of these individuals, their avoidant habit takes a serious emotional toll. The resulting isolation and loneliness are overwhelming, and their anger is turned inward. That pain becomes depression.

!! Dissatisfaction with life

Others never experience true depression but "lead lives of quiet desperation," to borrow a phrase from American writer Henry David Thoreau. They feel a general dissatisfaction with life. They feel something is missing. And something is! Like the other people we've just discussed, they're missing some of the emotional connection that comes from knowing and being known.

Think about it for a moment: if you're chronically unable to share your real thoughts and feelings, how can you ever feel loved and accepted for who you really are? This is certainly one of the many causes of the loneliness and disconnection that people experience in our culture today.

! *Occasional disconnection*

Of course, some people only feel this disconnection occasionally, but even that is unnecessary.

When we consider all the people in these various categories, when we consider both the mild cases as well as the more serious cases, we realize that just about everyone can suffer from conflict avoidance to some degree. We've probably all had times of biting our tongues but then stewing over our hurts or annoyances, and wondering what to do about them. All of us struggle occasionally with *when* to be assertive, and *how* to be assertive. We long to resolve conflict and live at peace, but we're not sure how to accomplish the goal.

So, what to do? Read on!

Questions: Barry's Story

1. How were conflict and differences of opinion handled in your family of origin?
2. This chapter lists five consequences of the avoidant environment, shown symbolically with one or more exclamation marks indicating the level of danger. Which ones, if any, have you seen within your family of origin?
3. As you observe your friends and coworkers, how do you see them handling conflict or differences of opinion?
4. How do you most often handle conflict or differences of opinion?

GUIDELINE A
Accept conflict as a good thing

Complete instruction in preventing and resolving conflict is beyond the scope of this book. However, I'm going to offer you some guidelines to get you started in the right direction. It's possible these guidelines will be enough to help you solve various concerns, but I don't know your situation and only you can decide what action is right for you at a certain time.

If you find yourself in any kind of trouble, I urge you to get help from a licensed counselor, a domestic violence shelter, or even your local law enforcement.

For more detailed instruction, I recommend you see Appendix A and study the books listed there, and then move on to more books. I also strongly urge you to join groups of people who want to grow and will keep you company along the way. This book can be used for group discussion and instruction. That's why role-play activities are included in Appendix B. So here are some general guidelines to get you started.

The first step for you may have already been accomplished—realizing that conflict is *not* always bad, and it should *not* be avoided routinely. In other words, the first step is recognizing the myth for what it is—a dangerous over-generalization. Of course, there will always be times when it is best to overlook an offense and say nothing. But we must reject the myth that encourages us to avoid conflict to an unhealthy degree.

Generally speaking, conflict is an opportunity for people to work out their differing desires, grow in character, cooperate with each other, and grow in mutual love and respect. Facing conflict or sharing diverse opinions is part of learning to love and learning to trust. In fact, as we've already seen, feeling free to share our true thoughts and feelings and receiving acceptance—and providing that acceptance for others in return—may be the key to our mental health.

Overcoming our fear of those conversations is one of the greatest gifts we can give to ourselves—and the people around us. As we change, we will encourage others to change with us. The change within us brings new energy and new life, a sense of being protected and a feeling of wellbeing, as gradually we learn there is nothing to fear.

Even when some nasty behavior comes at us, fundamental human desires usually lie at the root of the conflict—the desire to be valued, for example. We do better to view our so-called "difficult people" in this more sympathetic light and search for the underlying desires that are feeding the problem. We get much farther when we employ sympathetic eyes and a loving heart.

When we attempt to deal with conflict, sometimes a resolution is possible, and sometimes it is not. But no matter what, we gain tremendous benefits when we try. One benefit comes from speaking truth in love. Psychologically and morally, it is important for us to hear ourselves speaking truth.

Case Study: Hearing Ourselves Speak Truth

Mary's dad had often treated Mary rudely. As a child, on several occasions, she had cried alone in her room after enduring one of her dad's harsh comments. Now, as she is well into her adult years, Dad's angry responses and critical comments continue occasionally.

Recently, Mary went over to help her parents by doing yard work, but her chainsaw malfunctioned in the middle of cutting a tree branch. The saw obviously needed a tune-up. Rather than appreciate Mary's attempt to help and sympathize with her upcoming repair expense, Dad only criticized Mary's tool selection. Mary overheard her dad griping to another relative, "I knew that saw wouldn't cut that branch! I told her we should use something else!"

Her father's criticism stung, especially because the chainsaw was the perfect tool, if only it had been in working order. And her dad had been in no position to be able to predict the saw's failure. Dad's second-guessing Mary and then bad-mouthing her behind her back did not surprise her, but it still hurt. Because Mary had been working with a counselor on her own personal growth, she later spoke to her dad about the comments.

In a gentle and calm voice, she said, "Dad, I overheard your comments about me the other day regarding the chainsaw. I felt hurt that you were talking about me like that behind my back."

Her heart was pounding as she spoke, but she knew she was doing the right thing. Her dad never apologized and mumbled some vague denial, but Mary felt relieved that he did not explode, as the small child deep within her had feared. Mary was happy that she had accomplished her goal.

The goal in this case was not to hear an appropriate apology from her dad, though that would've been nice. The goal was not to hear her father cry out in anguish over how he had treated Mary all those years, though in a perfect world that would've happened at some point. The goal was more realistic. It was simply for Mary to control her own response and to communicate to her dad kindly but truthfully. She had spoken truth. And it was an important step in Mary's healing process. The healing power came from speaking truth, and from facing fears and destroying the old mental programming of a small child looking up at an angry and overpowering parent.

In other words, sometimes the *real* truth that we need to proclaim is this:

- my feelings do matter, or
- I do know what I'm talking about, or
- this isn't right.

Most of the time, we *won't* use those exact words and *shouldn't* use those words, because there are better, more effective ways of communicating. Mary, for example, never used those statements with her father. But these are the profoundly important underlying messages that shine through—the subtext, you might say. In Mary's case, her underlying message was that her feelings do matter and they're worth discussing. She needed to hear herself proclaim that message even more than her father needed to hear it. These profound messages shine light into our own hearts as well as the hearts of others.

Questions: Guideline A

1. Prior to reading this book, had you ever considered the idea of conflict as a good thing? How *have* you felt about conflict throughout your life?

2. What has been your past experience with speaking truth in love the way Mary did?

3. How would you summarize this chapter's message about the psychological, social, and moral benefits of having the courage to speak truth in love?

4. Can you describe more examples of how individuals and society in general could benefit if more people gathered the courage to speak truth in love?

GUIDELINE B
Benefit from I-statements

As you can tell from Mary's story, our words should be diplomatic and carefully chosen. One good option is to use what counselors call "I-statements." Look one more time at what Mary said to her dad:

"Dad, I overheard your comments about me the other day regarding the chainsaw. I felt hurt that you were talking about me like that behind my back."

Notice that Mary said "I overheard" and "I felt hurt." When we use I-statements, we speak for ourselves, and *only* for ourselves. No one can disagree with Mary's second statement and tell her she did not feel a certain way—although psychologically abusive people will try to shame others and say they *shouldn't* feel a certain way.

Regarding Mary's first I-statement, it's possible that we could mishear a comment, so someone could tell us that we didn't hear what we thought we heard. But the individual's pattern of behavior over time will help us to assess what's really happening in the relationship, regardless of what he or she might deny at a given time.

Using I-statements consistently is more difficult than we imagine. See? I just (purposely) violated the principle in this last sentence. If I were following the principle, I might write, "I believe that speaking only for ourselves is more difficult than we imagine."

Or better yet, "I don't know about you, but speaking only for myself is more difficult than I had imagined."

The fact is, I don't know what your experience is. I am, of course, just trying to make a general statement about a whole population for educational purposes. When we write anything lengthy that is designed to teach, we tend to drop "I think" or "I believe," because it becomes repetitive, and everyone understands that the whole message is designed to inform based upon (we hope) research.

But our relationships with other people, both at work and at home, will benefit from careful adherence to the principle as much as possible. It's just so hard to do sometimes.

One red flag occurs when we start a sentence with "you" rather than "I." Let's look at an example that varies depending on whether we're at work or at home. Imagine a supervisor at work saying each of these:

- "You should finish this job today," or
- "I would like you to finish this job today."

Of course, the tone of voice is always important, but let's just focus on word choice for a moment. Many people believe the second version sounds less bossy. They say that the word "you" sounds like a finger-pointing order, while the second option sounds softer. What do you think?

Now, let's consider both options being spoken in a husband-wife exchange:

- "You should finish this job today," or
- "I would like you to finish this job today."

If you believe the second one is better, is it good enough? Or do we need an even sweeter wording? Maybe, "Honey, I'm really hoping you can finish this today"? This sentence still qualifies as an I-statement because of the focus on how I—the speaker—feel. How does this last option strike you?

Let's look at another example. The question, "Would you like to go to a movie with me?" might really mean, "I would like you to go to a movie with me." If that's what we mean, we should say that, because there could be a significant difference between the two.

Say a wife asks her husband this question. He may feel legitimately confused. Is he merely being asked about his preferences? Or is he being asked to lovingly accommodate his wife's preference? Let's say her meaning is that she would like him to accommodate her desire. Then she should say some version of, "I'd love for you to go to a movie with me." This communication is more clear and will help the husband meet his wife's needs for companionship.

Here's a common example: "You're not listening to me!" This statement is more likely to cause defensiveness and arguments because it is a blaming statement. "I don't feel listened to right now" is an indisputable fact that you own. If that's how you feel, then that's how you feel. No one else can tell you how you feel—though boundary-crossers will try!

Perhaps you'll say I'm splitting hairs here, that the distinction has no value because the recipient of either remark will still feel blamed. I agree that it takes time to modify the dynamics between people. When we change this surface communication, we're also in the process of changing two things:

1. our habit of having a blaming attitude
2. the way others interpret our comments.

It takes time to shift the dynamics between two people, especially when there's a history of difficulty. But as we use I-statements more and more, the philosophy behind the I-statements will begin to take hold:

- we take more responsibility for the way we feel, which can be quite independent of what the other person is doing,
- we recognize a broad concept known as "healthy boundaries," which includes becoming clear on what is and is not our responsibility,
- and we focus on solutions rather than blaming.

So, when we use the proper phrasing, the question becomes, *what can the other person do to help us feel more listened to?* Maybe we all need to slow down, eliminate distractions, focus attention on one another, be more understanding, and think more about what everyone needs. It's also extremely helpful to show we understand what the other person is saying. We'll cover that later in the chapter on empathy. Empathy is an important part of communicating. The importance of empathy cannot be overstated, and that's why I'm committed to teaching those communication skills.

In short, speaking for ourselves with I-statements helps to bypass arguments and move to solutions. The biggest challenge for many of us is that we were never trained to speak in I-statements. We're more likely, in the preceding example, to say, "You're not listening to me!"

We must train ourselves in a new two-step process:

- make sure we're aware of what we're really thinking, feeling, and wanting, and then
- express that clearly and specifically.

All of this is a matter of working to change our daily habits. The benefits include more harmonious relationships at work and at home, less confusion and conflict, greater productivity at work, and so much more.

We could all commit to practicing I-statements—or *recommit* to practicing if we've already heard about them. We could observe how long we can stick with I-statements in a given conversation. Oh, and just in case somebody needs this reminder—we've already covered speaking truth in love. So your I-statements shouldn't be things like:

- "I think you are a jerk," or
- "I feel so depressed because I'm stuck with a _____ like you."

Yeah, I know. There goes that great feeling of satisfaction that comes from giving someone both barrels when they deserve it most. I have to ruin everything, don't I? But seriously, we win when we control our tongue.

Instead of being provoked and making things worse and feeling lousy about ourselves deep down, we can start using the formula, "When you do X, I feel Y, and what I'd like in the future is Z."

X is the specific behavior. Often, we'll use this formula to describe hurtful or annoying behaviors, but we can use this formula for pleasing behaviors too.

Y is the emotion—sad, hurt, angry, confused, happy, relieved, excited, etc.

Z is the specific desired behavior. It could be that we're asking for an improvement of some kind. Or, if we're describing how happy we are, the Z we're asking for might be more of the same.

We don't always have to use that formula, but it can help to think about a formula when we're starting out. We'll quickly develop our own variations. Sometimes, we'll just cover the X and the Y, and save the Z for a brainstorming session with the other person. Sometimes, we'll start with only the "I feel Y" and let the conversation flow naturally from there. Sometimes, our I-statements don't deal with feelings at all, only opinions and thoughts. As we gradually get into the habit of speaking for ourselves, we'll become more and more comfortable using I-statements in all their variations.

Questions: Guideline B

1. Prior to reading this book, had you heard of I-statements? If so, have you tried using them? How did that go?
2. I used the phrase "psychologically abusive" to describe people who tell us that we shouldn't feel a certain way. Does that wording seem too strong to you? Why or why not?
3. I used the phrase "boundary crossers" to describe person A trying to tell person B how B feels. Why is that considered "crossing a boundary"?

GUIDELINE C
Cultivate outer and inner calm

Perhaps you also noticed from Mary's story that it's important to use a calm and loving tone of voice. Our ultimate goal is not only to show that calm on the outside, but also to feel it on the inside. But even if that peacefulness is accomplished, rest assured that we could be creating a profound impact.

As I mentioned earlier, sometimes the subtext message is:

- my feelings do matter, or
- I do know what I'm talking about, or
- this isn't right.

These profound, underlying messages, these declarations of independence, ring out with great shouts of freedom—freedom to value our own feelings and opinions, freedom to speak truth no matter what, freedom from a crippling fear of the other person's response. And our calm demeanor adds to this power rather than diminishing it. That's worth repeating: our calm demeanor adds to our power rather than diminishing it.

We'd probably all agree that cultivating that outer and inner calm is overwhelmingly difficult at times. For years, I couldn't do it. I searched for a solution. I failed repeatedly. Sometimes my indignation showed, and I came on too strong and made things worse. Sometimes my fear and emotional pain showed, and they were misinterpreted as aggression. Finally, I learned to step out in faith and stop relying on others for approval. That gave me the strength I needed to stay calm, at least on the outside. But it wasn't easy. Sometimes we realize we have two choices—allow ourselves to be destroyed or decide God's opinion of us is the only one that counts. I chose the latter, and that allowed me to develop outer and inner calm.

I like to say it was like giving up an addiction—in this case an addiction to the approval of others. And I am still working to get away from that addiction, still working on keeping the inner calm each time a new challenge comes along. It may be a lifelong process, as I gradually grow stronger and stronger. Growth takes time.

So here's one thing I know: even when the other people in our world disappoint us or abandon us, we can still experience a great and glorious victory and attain peace despite the pain.

However, when other people do respond appropriately and the issue is resolved, life is even sweeter. We often can gain a greater closeness in the relationship and a greater sense of being loved or respected. Then our wrongdoers have learned to become better people. Perhaps they have been saved from their ignorance about how they were coming across. Or perhaps they always knew they were in the wrong, but needed some accountability to straighten up. Either way, we make the world a better place when we help them change and grow. And because life always hands out consequences for bad behavior sooner or later, our constructive feedback might spare them some future misery—*if* they will listen.

Case Study: Offering Feedback

Emily was house hunting and found one old house for sale that seemed to be an amazing buy. It was sitting empty and the owner was in a nursing home with dementia. No one knew much about the house.

When the listing agent, Marsha, showed her the house, Emily saw that the oak floor was crumbling in one spot near the front door—evidence of past termite damage. *No problem*, she thought. That could be repaired. And a termite inspection would let her know that the termites were a thing of the past.

So later that day, she met Marsha's assistant, Juan, to write the offer. She wrote into the contract that her offer was subject to her own subsequent inspections plus professional inspections.

Emily noticed how much time the paperwork took, and she expressed sympathy to Juan for the time realtors have to spend showing houses and writing offers. Juan was gracious about it, and Emily left the office thinking she would work with Juan for future house hunting if this house failed an inspection.

Later that same night, Emily did some Internet research on termite damage. She read about wood floors and how termite activity can cause a slightly water-damaged look in addition to actual holes. She realized the floors she'd seen had that look almost everywhere.

She read about the need to tear into the walls to look for structural damage in the more severe cases. She suddenly recalled how every room in the house had a change in the walls—the original plaster was long gone and cheap wallboard had been used in a couple of the rooms. Did the house still have structural damage? The articles said the only way to know for sure would be to tear into the walls again.

She read about the hazardous nature of the chemical treatments. And she read warnings about the stigma that termite-damaged houses can carry, making them almost impossible to sell.

Emily texted both Marsha and Juan to let them know she was canceling the contract. Marsha apparently thought her reply would go only to Juan when she texted back, "Add her to our crazy list. What a waste of time on a Saturday!"

When Emily saw the text, she felt wounded and sad about Marsha's disregard for her. She decided to speak up and kindly let Marsha know she was aware of her attitude. She also wanted to present another option to Marsha. Because she thought she would not have a chance to speak with Marsha face-to-face, and because she wanted Juan to see her response also, she texted back:

"Marsha, I would've preferred you'd do the ethical thing and tell me the wall and flooring changes suggested major infestation. Or if you couldn't due to an ethical obligation to your seller, you'd at least show understanding for me once I decided to protect myself. I was thinking I'd work with Juan for future house hunting. But now you and your team have lost that business. Kindness always comes back to you somehow."

Apparently, Marsha didn't understand the concept of kindness coming back to her and the power of word-of-mouth advertising, or maybe she was planning to be gracious to Emily's face while secretly demeaning her. That would also cost Marsha in the long run. Who likes a two-faced hypocrite?

Apparently, Marsha's view was simply that Emily should make a bad purchase so that she and her team could get their commission.

Apparently, she didn't think Emily deserved the same rights she'd want for herself. Marsha was in the wrong, and yet she called Emily "crazy."

In order to protect their egos, wrongdoers often blame the other party—in this case calling Emily "crazy." When we are attacked as Emily was, especially by people who are close to us, it's easy for us to feel shame. No matter what we tell ourselves in our head, our heart can sometimes feel the shame.

Emily could have said nothing, could have acted as if she had never seen that text. But whom would she have helped? She is now less likely to feel resentment and bitterness because she has chosen to speak truth in love. And she had a shot at helping Marsha become a better human being and businessperson. Maybe the shock and embarrassment of being exposed like that would cause Marsha to change the way she treats customers. Who knows?

It's worth emphasizing—resolution is not always possible. Many people do not *want* to improve. But as we've discussed, the benefits of speaking truth are also for us. And the benefits are also for others who might be affected, whether they are future customers, or coworkers, or children in the family, or other members of a group.

And still, so many people in our culture preach conflict avoidance:

- "Just get along!" or
- "Don't say anything! Just bear everything in love."

In most settings, when we challenge one another and spur each other on to greater character and better behavior, we are protecting the health and the unity of the group long term. And we are helping to improve the entire society.

Questions: Guideline C

1. In the past, have you worked on assertiveness and remaining calm during difficult conversations? What's been your experience with navigating those types of conversations?
2. If you had been in Emily's position, what would you have done when you saw that text message calling you "crazy"?
3. How do you feel about the idea of providing feedback to others so that they can improve?
4. What would happen if everyone refused to provide corrective feedback to others?

GUIDELINE D
Develop the strength for humility

As you learned about Emily's attempt to influence Marsha's behavior, maybe it became clear that *humility* is the key to everyone's success.

Humility is that ability to look upon our own faults and mistakes and feel a desire to improve. Humility *wants* feedback. Humility *welcomes* criticism—but hopes it is delivered in a kind way! We need others to show us humility, and we need to show the same to them.

Some leaders of families or organizations or governments try to put themselves above having to listen to any kind of feedback or constructive criticism. They may want to ban truth spoken in love. Perhaps, if we examined their past history, we'd see someone severely wounded from too many mean-spirited criticisms! Anyone who has been a leader for very long knows that some people can be horribly critical and insensitive, and these people have no one's best interests at heart.

Nevertheless, despite the pain and special challenges of leadership, humility is important even for leaders. In fact, real power, real influence, comes from humility. And real strength demonstrates humility.

The bottom line is this: everything I am writing about depends upon the spirit with which correction is offered and the spirit with which it is received. A humble attitude is the key for everyone.

This is where believing it's okay to be a work-in-progress kicks in. When we truly accept ourselves as a work-in-progress, when we *really* decide that's okay, then we become strong enough to take some criticism or suggestions for improvement. Of course we have areas that need improvement! We're human, aren't we?

When we truly get this understanding into our core self-concept, we're no longer so wounded, no longer so defensive if someone finds fault with us. When our critics are right, we'll admit it.

Here's a Bible verse that applies: "The truth shall set you free."

I think it's partly proclaiming the same idea I've been trying to convey—when you understand you are a child of God and you are loved even with your flaws, then truth is no longer a scary thing. Rather, it becomes your best friend.

So in this case, where we're discussing criticism, there's no need to fear the criticism any longer. If it is valid, then it helps you course-correct. If it is wrong (and perhaps even unfair and mean-spirited), then it possibly gives you useful insight about the person who is delivering that criticism to you. Either way, you've gained useful information.

So now, when our critics are wrong, or when there's another way of looking at the situation, we can kindly let them know. They deserve a response. But when there is a bit of truth there, we can thank them for their input, and mean it sincerely.

We're strong. We're not weak and reacting defensively out of pride. When you're strong, defending yourself isn't the main goal. When you're strong, the truth is what matters most. And you're not afraid of it.

Questions: Guideline D

1. Some people might consider "humility" an old-fashioned term. But how have you been affected by a lack of humility in others?

2. What does this sentence mean to you—"real power, real influence, comes from humility"?

3. What about this sentence—"real strength demonstrates humility"?

4. I happen to believe that the unwillingness of many people to acknowledge their own mistakes and faults is the number-one cause of destroyed or strained relationships. Do you agree or disagree, and why?

GUIDELINE E
Examine your actions or inaction

Using that strength and that humility, we can then mentally review the history to see if we contributed somehow to the conflict. In daily life, it is hard to avoid contributing in some way. That's because we have our own vulnerabilities, our moments of impatience, and so on. And in addition to all of that, we also lack the ability to read the other person's mind. Sometimes as we look back, we realize we couldn't have known what would've helped a situation, but we're glad to know now.

All of these human weaknesses and limitations are understandable. All we can do is cultivate an eagerness to know what could have helped, so that we can make use of the information later.

There are times, if we're going to get honest with ourselves, that we have to admit our actions helped to create the conflict or confusion or whatever. Or, maybe it was our *inaction*—our failure to act—that added to the problem. Again, if we can hold onto the understanding that it's okay to be a work-in-progress, then we can face the truth that we may have contributed to the problem.

In a rare situation, we can be completely innocent of any mistake or wrongdoing. Let's look at an example of that.

Case Study: Being 100% innocent

At work, a supervisor was jealous of Karen's personal qualities and abilities and began to mistreat her. He would snap at her in annoyance when she asked a legitimate question. He would assign her tasks knowing they were beyond her current ability level. He would mock her in front of others.

Maybe you've encountered this type of boss. If so, you know how miserable it can be. Karen "took the high road," as they say. She never snapped back. She never reacted to the mistreatment. She didn't start to withdraw and ignore him, which would eventually annoy him and inflame the situation. Karen never failed to follow instructions—she did not resort to rebellion or passive resistance. She never complained about him to others. She had never even made a statement that was confusing or unclear, so she had not even added to any confusion. She hadn't done a single thing to contribute to the problem.

Karen is a good example of an ideal response. But many times, we just can't manage to achieve that standard. So, as we mentally review a situation, let's remember to consider this list of common mistakes:

! Unclear communication

Sometimes we contribute to conflict, even if we weren't aware of it at the time. Looking back at what went wrong, we might need to at least accept responsibility for unclear communication and adding to the confusion, if confusion is part of the problem. It's not hard to own up to and apologize for unclear communication, is it?

!! Avoidance

In a conflict situation, we might need to acknowledge that we've begun to respond with avoidance—pulling away, ignoring, or shunning the offender. It can be really hard to distinguish between pulling back to create some safe boundaries and pulling back as an inappropriate avoidance strategy that rejects and annoys the offender even more. Recognizing the difference in our own behavior can be quite a challenge!

Whether your offenders know it or not, deep down, they would probably have you confront them and speak truth in love, rather than ignore them and shun them. After all, remember that famous saying, "The opposite of love is not hate; it's indifference"? When we feel some connection to other people, sometimes we would rather have them upset with us than completely ignoring us.

Need some proof? Look at the behavior of children when feeling ignored by a parent: they prefer to misbehave and incur the parent's wrath rather than settle for being completely ignored and feeling abandoned. Likewise, many married couples fight to maintain an emotional connection and get attention. In their minds, whether they're conscious of this or not, the fighting beats the alternative—that feeling of complete disconnection. Engaging in battles can serve as an antidote to loneliness, although it's an unhealthy antidote. Even in relationships that are less intimate than family relationships, people can feel pain when they see others pulling away.

So, we can make things much worse if we give in to a natural tendency to pull away from an offender without first having conducted the proper steps of conflict resolution.

!!! Passive resistance/passive aggression

Some of us might also have to engage in a painful gut check and admit that we've begun to passively resist the offender. Did we begin to act like Barry, "forgetting" to do a particular task, or otherwise failing to do the things we should have done? Did we start to put out less effort?

!!!! Aggression

And finally, would we admit that we've begun to retaliate in some other way besides passive resistance? Have we perhaps retaliated by gossiping about the offender? Have we retaliated tit-for-tat? "He snaps at me; I snap right back at him." That can be extremely difficult to avoid in personal relationships. I hope we wouldn't retaliate with an even greater measure: "He snaps at me; I key his car and smash in the windows!"

As we've already noted, Karen is an example of an ideal response. Obviously, when our lives are threatened or something dangerous is happening, a sudden escape may be best. And as we already learned, there are situations at the other end of the spectrum that simply call for us to overlook the offense, let it go, and say nothing. But in many ordinary situations, staying near the person and not retaliating but speaking truth in love is the best way to go, not just because it's "right" but because it also might produce the best results.

So Karen will need to have a talk with her supervisor, and her behavior up to that point has laid some excellent groundwork for the discussion. She has not compounded the problem with her own wrongdoing. She has not added fuel to the fire. She is on solid ground for proceeding. If she had committed any of the offenses described above, she might begin by apologizing to her supervisor for those imperfect responses. She would own her side of the ledger, thus humbling herself, setting a great example of humility for her supervisor, disarming him with her confession, and providing a transition to the topic of *his* behavior toward *her*.

As you can tell from the mention of "disarming" the other person, these kinds of wise responses constitute great strategy as well. But they don't work if they're just insincere manipulation. They only work when they arise out of character and integrity. When you face someone in a conflict resolution conversation, your character will be tested. What kind of inner strength will you display? The inner strength you need is not a tough-guy approach. The inner strength you need comes from knowing who you are and whether you're prepared for the battle with a willingness to care for other people, even *with* all their annoying traits.

Questions: Guideline E

1. Imagine you own the company where Karen works. What are all the ways that Karen's supervisor is jeopardizing your financial success?

2. This chapter contains a list of common mistakes that we make that contribute to conflict. Which one is bothering you the most in other people's behavior?

3. Which one would you make top priority for change and improvement within yourself?

GUIDELINE F
Find a wise approach

We benefit by using wisdom when facing relationship challenges.

First, we should guard against jumping to the opposite of conflict avoidance—patrolling all our relationships and calling people out for every little offense. We don't need to speak up every single time we disagree with someone or feel slightly miffed over a comment. We're more effective when we evaluate carefully.

Second, we can exhibit patience. Sometimes, waiting a few days can help us decide whether an issue is that important. And it's good to avoid snap decisions when we're feeling tired, hungry, or lonely. A waiting period is also useful for taking time to seek wise advice and plan the conversation.

The kind of advisor you'll consult depends, of course, on the situation. For some upcoming conversations, you might only prepare with some relaxation, meditation, and prayer—no human advisor at all. For other situations, you might consult a mentor or counselor or spiritual leader. For anything more serious, you might avoid interaction with that person completely, and your advisors could become a domestic violence advocate, police department, lawyer, insurance agent, or some other professional.

Third, we can do a careful analysis. As we evaluate the situation and make our plan, we can ask ourselves if this is a first occasion, or whether a pattern has developed. We can consider the type of relationship. How often do we see this person? How much do we depend upon this person? How well do we know the person? What background information do we have for interpreting the situation correctly? What is our highest goal for this relationship? Will a conversation help us achieve that goal? What are the possible ways the other person might react? What does past evidence suggest is most likely? What risks are we willing to take? We should consider all of these factors.

Fourth, if and when we're ready to proceed with the conversation, we can employ good timing. What's the mood of the other person at this time? Would a later time be better? Are there major distractions occurring that could be avoided later?

Fifth, we can also employ the proper method. Assuming it's safe and advisable to initiate a conversation, personal conversations generally yield the best results when done in person. A face-to-face meeting allows the other person to receive our nonverbal communication, which includes our facial expressions, tone of voice, body posture, and so on.

When we can't meet in person, a video conference may be second best and a phone call would be next, followed by the most dangerous option—written communication, which includes email, phone text, social media messages, and paper letters.

Written communication is risky because people can't hear the tone of voice and often tend to imagine a more hostile message than what's intended. There is also no immediate opportunity for clarifying the intended meaning, and so misunderstandings are a common result. One good rule of thumb to remember is, "Never put negative stuff into writing."

In summary, it might be helpful to use this checklist when we're planning our approach:

- Is this something I need to address at all?
- Should I wait to cool off and take time to ponder?
- Am I extra vulnerable right now due to tiredness, loneliness or hunger?
- Have I sought wise advice and planned this out with careful analysis?
- Am I picking a good time and place and method of approach?

The bottom line is simply this: being patient and finding a wise approach can mean the difference between success and failure.

Questions: Guideline F

1. It's so tempting for me, and perhaps for everyone, to deliver disappointing news or criticism in writing vs. doing so face-to-face. And yet, we know that we might be jeopardizing our success and our relationships when we hide behind the written word, hoping for more comfort and safety. How have you tended to handle these situations in the past—at work and at home? What were the outcomes?

2. How have you been doing with selecting the proper timing for a difficult conversation? Can you recall some specific examples?

3. Have you ever tried the pre-analysis described in this chapter? Did that help things go better?

GUIDELINE G
Give empathy

This guideline may be the most important of all. Empathy is the ability to see the perspective of others, understand their feelings, and then *express* that understanding with compassion. This one communication skill is almost magical in its power to help people bond, reduce conflict, heal emotionally, and so much more—plus, it even makes you a great conversationalist!

It is the opposite of immediately switching to talking about yourself. If only more people would learn that! Someone once told me she thought her constant switching to talking about her own experience was a way of connecting. Yes, there are times when it's useful to give a bit of one's own autobiography, but doing that before the empathy has been given, and doing it constantly, especially after being educated on this topic, speaks to a toxic obsession with self, and it does tremendous damage to other people, regardless of whether or not those people recognize the problem.

I have experienced the amazing benefits of empathy, both as a recipient and as a giver.

Showing empathy mostly comes down to a practical skill that I teach, which often amounts to paraphrasing back to the person in a kind, understanding, and compassionate manner what he or she just said. Showing empathy also includes acknowledging the other person's emotions, when emotion is present. To those who are not aware of the power of this kind of response, rephrasing what the other has said may seem silly and pointless. And showing awareness of another's feelings may seem intrusive. But as I said, the effect is almost magical.

One reason this skill is so valuable is that we humans have a tremendous psychological need to feel heard and understood. When that need is met—which is all too rare in our culture—we feel so much better. I call this technique "The Reflective Response," and you can learn exactly how to do it by completing my workshop by the same name.

This skill might be ineffective if we don't follow some of our other guidelines—cultivating calm, examining our contribution to the problem, understanding our worth is not determined by this other person, having a heart of compassion, and so on. Our fundamental attitudes show when we're dealing with others. People will be able to sense whether we're warm or cold. If you suspect you're a little frosty around the heart, working on the guidelines will help to warm you up. Your desire to find success in life, your desire to be the best you can be, will prevail if you truly give your heart to finding the Narrow Gate.

Questions: Guideline G

1. Have you ever felt that release of tension as you received empathy and felt understood? What was the that like for you?
2. Have you ever used empathy to restore calm in a high-conflict situation? What happened?
3. How can you employ ideas from this chapter in your day-to-day life?

The Better Path, More Ideas

Once we understand the guidelines outlined in this book, we're ready to grow even more as a person, develop our character even more, which will, in turn, bring us even more peace and comfort.

You can make more progress with all of the following:

- the books listed in Appendix A
- more books that you find later
- the ongoing counsel of a wise advisor
- group support and practice (see Appendix B)
- continued spiritual development.

All of these resources will help you map out more specific plans for any situation you want to improve.

As you are probably beginning to see, finding the Narrow Gate involves some extra effort on your part, and that's one reason why some people wander through the wide gate. Maybe they're too lazy to put forth the effort. Or maybe they've never realized that the wiser options are available to them. That can happen when we are swept along by the crowd and are too distracted to realize there's another path. But really, the misery that comes from remaining ignorant is much too big a price to pay. No one would knowingly choose the wide gate, not if he or she knew what was waiting farther down the road. All that misery and unhappiness is so unnecessary.

It's good to bear in mind that voicing your thoughts and feelings is a daily lifestyle opportunity. It's not just a problem-*solving* strategy: it's also a problem-*preventing* strategy. Speaking truth in love prevents the build-up of frustration and anger, and that should translate into fewer relationship strains, fewer breakups, less depression, and even less of the pathology we saw in Barry.

It bears repeating that, if you're in a dangerous situation, you should seek help and save many of these ideas for a later time. Your source of help, once again, might be a licensed counselor, domestic violence shelter, your local police, a lawyer, or any other professional that is needed in your situation.

But for other situations, speaking truth in love on a regular basis—and learning to do it well—is a way to grow and help others grow. It is uplifting and energizing. When you are free from the fear of speaking truth, you can feel both soothed and exhilarated. Those early successes can feel like breaking out of prison. A horrible weight comes off your chest, and you can finally breathe freely, and you like the new you.

The key is learning the skills you need to handle the conversation well, along with practicing the proper spiritual disciplines. Otherwise, if you rely only on skill without the heart being right, your success will be limited—if it happens at all. I speak from experience! That's why it's so important to go slowly, learn carefully, analyze, and prepare your heart. Then you can look forward to engaging with people in a way that brings a blanket of comfort around your heart, and you'll feel alive and aware of the beauty and grandeur of life.

But be forewarned: even when your skills and preparation are adequate, if you're with toxic people, you'll likely receive pushback for speaking truth in love. No matter how well coached our communication is, toxic people may still shame us and apply tremendous pressure to get us to shut up and go back to living life their way. The more toxic they are, the more severe their threats will be. That's when we make extra, *extra* sure that we are using every available source of wisdom, double-checking our own contributions to the problem, making sure we are spiritually on solid ground.

Even in situations that are not toxic, I still urge you to avoid the "lone ranger" role. Reach out for all the sources of help that you can, and proceed slowly and cautiously. Make the effort to treat your life as the masterpiece it is meant to be. Seek the path of Wisdom, and take good care of yourself.

Though normally we would hate to experience such a nasty reaction from a toxic person, there is an upside to it. The greater the battle, the greater your reward will be. If you are taking responsibility for your own mistakes first and apologizing for them, if you are proceeding with love and wisdom, if you have tapped into all the sources of wide guidance that I've mentioned, if you are proceeding in the best way possible, and you still receive nasty opposition, then you also have a measure of the kind of damage you're enduring as you suffer silently and say nothing—and probably the damage that others in the group are enduring. And you have a measure of the potential improvement that could come from a loving application of truth.

In other words, we can view the nasty pushback we receive as research data to be gathered, rather than a devastating blow that crushes us. This research data is helping us define the problem, plumb the depths of the dysfunction, and figure out where we really are and how to proceed. When we're seeking Wisdom and doing our best, life is good, no matter what. And we can learn to rise above our difficult circumstances.

Questions: The Better Path

1. Consider this statement: "It's good to bear in mind that voicing your thoughts and feelings is a daily lifestyle opportunity. It's not just a problem-*solving* strategy. It's also a problem-*preventing* strategy." Can you give specific examples in your own daily life of how voicing your thoughts and feelings might help to prevent problems? Or can you think of some hypothetical examples?

2. Have you ever received "pushback" from "toxic people" as a result of speaking truth in love? What ideas in this book can help with that in the future?

Conclusion

There might be people in your life who shame you when you want to have a thoughtful discussion. I'm thinking of the types who laugh off everything, tell us we take things too seriously. They tend to be the same types who brag that they don't let anything bother them, which of course implies they're superior. Those are all lies, of course.

If we're going to find the Narrow Gate, we'll have to stop worrying about their approval. They're sold on the wide gate and the broad road, and they're heading for pain and misery, if they're not already there. Perhaps they want you to join them—or stay with them—and perhaps that's because they'll feel better about themselves if you self-destruct, too, right along with them. Maybe you're no longer interested in pleasing people like that—if you ever were.

I hope this book will help you avoid much of the pain and misery so many others have experienced. You may have learned something new, or just gained encouragement for changing the direction of your life.

Perhaps now you can see how conflict and loving confrontation can be a blessing and an opportunity for a better life for everyone.

Goodbye, Myth #1.

We are on a growth path, and I hope you're fired up about reclaiming the happiness you were born to enjoy. God bless you every step of the way!

APPENDIX A
Recommended Reading

I am purposely keeping this list short. Why? In today's culture, we are overloaded with information and choices, but I believe we learn best through a concise progression of ideas. I'd like to save you the work of wading through a long list and trying to decide which book to pick. Anytime you desire, you can search for more titles and extend your knowledge.

Remember that I strongly encourage you to seek wise counsel in addition to any reading that you do, but here are my recommendations:

How To Have That Difficult Conversation You've Been Avoiding: With Your Spouse, Adult Child, Family, Boss, Coworker, Friend, Parent, or Someone You're Dating, by Dr. Henry Cloud and Dr. John Townsend.

There are many, many books that talk *about* the problems or challenges of life, and many that talk specifically about conflict resolution, but this one is written in a plain, easy-to-read style and also gives you many examples of exactly what to say.

The *Boundaries* books, also by Dr. Henry Cloud and Dr. John Townsend.

There is the regular *Boundaries*, plus *Boundaries in Marriage*, *Boundaries in Dating*, and *Boundaries with Kids*.

APPENDIX B
Role-Play Activities for Groups

Have fun practicing I-statements aloud with a partner. You can either use real examples or invent some. Begin by using the full formula. Once you're comfortable with the full formula, begin trying the variations described at the end of section about Guideline B.

Example: Someone borrowed from you and hasn't returned the item.

> "[Name], when you borrow my things and fail to return them, I feel disappointed and annoyed. I'd like you to return this latest item as soon as possible."

Here are some other prompts in case you need them:

1. Someone borrowed a specific item from you and broke it beyond repair. What request will you include in your formula I-statement?
2. Someone has lied to you, and you just caught the lie.
3. Someone has a habit of making plans with you but often cancels on short notice for no good reason.
4. Someone keeps leaving trash in your car after borrowing it or riding with you.
5. Someone is habitually late and holds up the group meeting. You are the group leader, so this is your problem to handle.

About the Author

Carol Diane is on a mission to free everyone from the dysfunctional ideas in modern culture and help people of all ages reclaim the happiness they were meant to enjoy. She has a master's degree in counseling and a bachelor's degree in communication. She has been a counselor, teacher, chaplain assistant, tutor, homeschooler, and more. Most of what she teaches is applicable in marriage, parenting, other family relationships, friendships, coworker relationships, management, sales, customer service, committee work, mediation, crisis response, mentoring, coaching, counseling, ministry, and more. She is known for her care and compassion and desire to help people succeed in whatever they wish to accomplish.

Made in United States
Cleveland, OH
18 November 2025